_____

(name)

has read

The Surprise Inside

story summary to me.

_____

(signed)

The Surprise Inside

story summary

Red,
green,

yellow,

blue,

pink,
orange,

purple.
Boo!

_____

(name)

has read the

Our School

story summary to me.

_____

(signed)

Our School

story summary

Our School

our school

6

our teacher

3

our classroom

our table

our books

our work

_____

(name)

has read the

Up, Down, Round and Round

story summary to me.

_____

(signed)

Up, Down, Round and Round

story summary

Up, down, round and round.

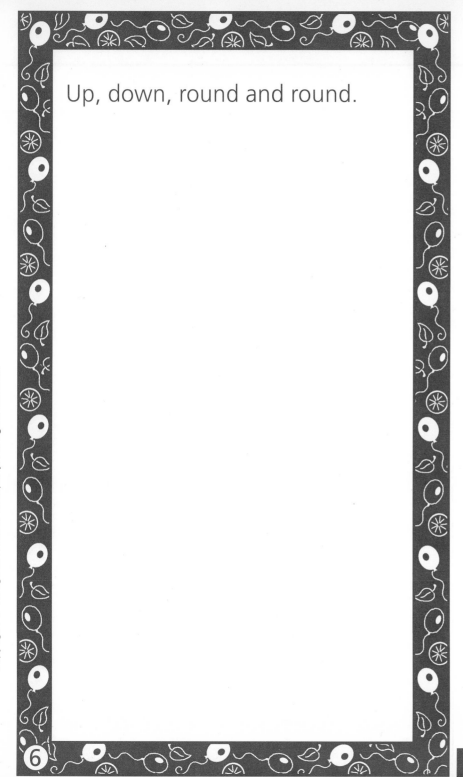

Up, down, round and round.

6

A balloon goes up.

A kite goes up.

3

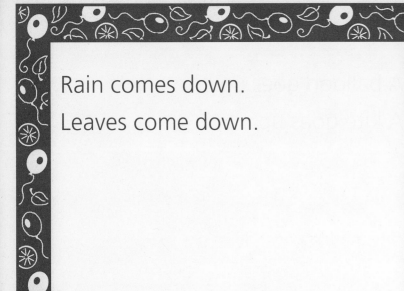

Rain comes down.

Leaves come down.

Carousels go round and round.

_____

(name)

has read the

Breakfast

story summary to me.

_____

(signed)

Breakfast

story summary

I squeeze an orange.

I make breakfast!

I butter bread.

I pour milk.

I crack an egg.

_____

(name)

has read the

Carlos

story summary to me.

_____

(signed)

Carlos

story summary

one sister

five fingers

two grandmothers

⑥

③

three freckles

four friends

4

5

_____

(name)

has read the

Pumpkins

story summary to me.

_____

(signed)

Pumpkins

story summary

A seed grows in the ground.

A pumpkin can become
pumpkin pie or
a Jack-o'-Lantern!

A vine grows from the seed.

The vine has flowers.

And soon the pumpkins grow.

4

5

_____

(name)

has read the

Firefighters!

story summary to me.

_____

(signed)

Firefighters!

story summary

There's a fire!

Get ready for another fire.

6

27

Hurry! Put it out!

3

Water! Water!

The fire is out.

_____

(name)

has read

The Mockingbird

story summary to me.

_____

(signed)

The Mockingbird

story summary

The mockingbird sings
in the morning.

The mockingbird sings
for everyone.

6

The mockingbird sings
in the sun.

3

The mockingbird sings
in the evening.

The mockingbird sings
when day is done.

_____

(name)

has read the

Summertime

story summary to me.

_____

(signed)

Summertime

story summary

I feel wind in my hair,

and sun on my back.
Summer!

6

sand between my toes,

3

salt on my lips,

waves on my legs,

_____

(name)

has read the

On the Farm

story summary to me.

_____

(signed)

On the Farm

story summary

I went to a farm one day.

What do you think I saw?

What do you think I heard?

②

Now you say it, too.

Oink. Oink. Oink.

Baa. Baa. Baa.

Moo. Moo. Moo.

6

I saw a pig.

I heard it say,

Oink, oink, oink.

3

I saw a sheep.

I heard it say,

Baa, baa, baa.

④

I saw a cow.

I heard it say,

Moo, moo, moo.

⑤

_____

(name)

has read the

After a Bath

story summary to me.

_____

(signed)

After a Bath

story summary

After a bath, I dry myself.

If I were a dog, I'd take less time.
I could shake myself dry!

6

43

I wipe my hands
and my fingers.

3

I wipe my legs
and my toes.

I wipe my shiny nose,
and I'm dry!

_____

(name)

has read the

An Elephant's Trunk

story summary to me.

_____

(signed)

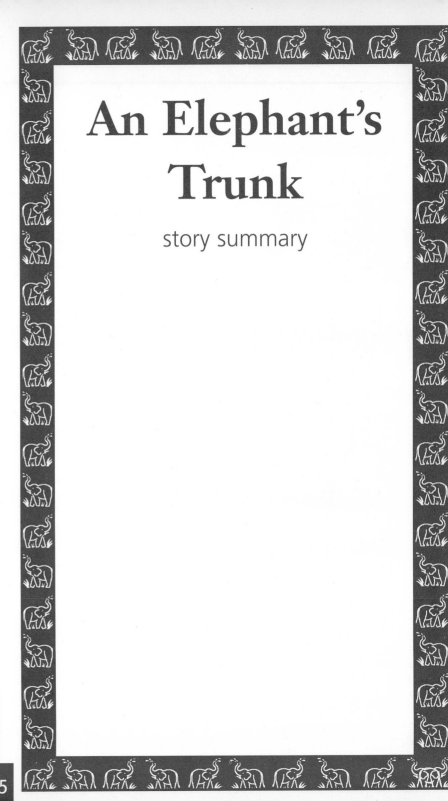

An Elephant's Trunk

story summary

and for holding onto a friend!

6

47

An elephant's trunk is
for smelling, for breathing,

3

for lifting, for reaching,

for drinking, for taking a shower,

_____

(name)

has read the

Teacher's Pet

story summary to me.

_____

(signed)

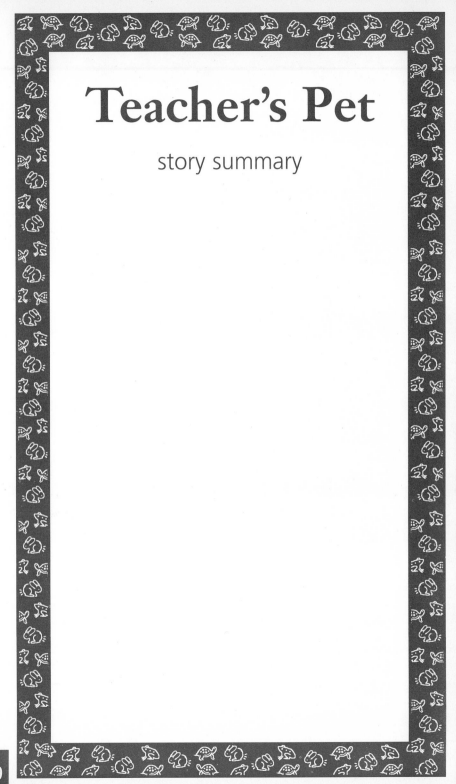

Teacher's Pet

story summary

It looks like a zoo!

Carla's caterpillar, and
Fred's frog!

⑥

Rose's rabbit,
Cathy's cat,

③

Wayne's hamster,

Bobby's rat,

Tam's turtle,

David's dog,

_____

(name)

has read the

When Grandpa Visits

story summary to me.

_____

(signed)

When Grandpa Visits

story summary

When Grandpa visits,
he hangs his clothes here
and I hang my clothes there.

And so do I!

6

55

He puts his toothbrush here
and I put my toothbrush there.

3

He sleeps there
and I sleep here.

When Grandpa visits,
he reads here.

_____

(name)

has read the

Iguana

story summary to me.

_____

(signed)

Iguana

story summary

What do iguanas like?

And the iguana in my yard
likes me!

They like sunshine
and warm rocks.

They like flowers and leaves and fruit.

They like to climb trees.

_____

(name)

has read

The Tiny Dot

story summary to me.

_____

(signed)

The Tiny Dot

story summary

The tiny dot on the leaf is an egg.

and out comes a butterfly!

When the egg hatches,
a caterpillar comes out.

Then the caterpillar spins
a cocoon.

The cocoon opens,

_____

(name)

has read the

Busy Week

story summary to me.

_____

(signed)

Busy Week

story summary

1

Monday

I have Brownie club.

2

Tuesday

I have gym.

I wish the week was eight days!

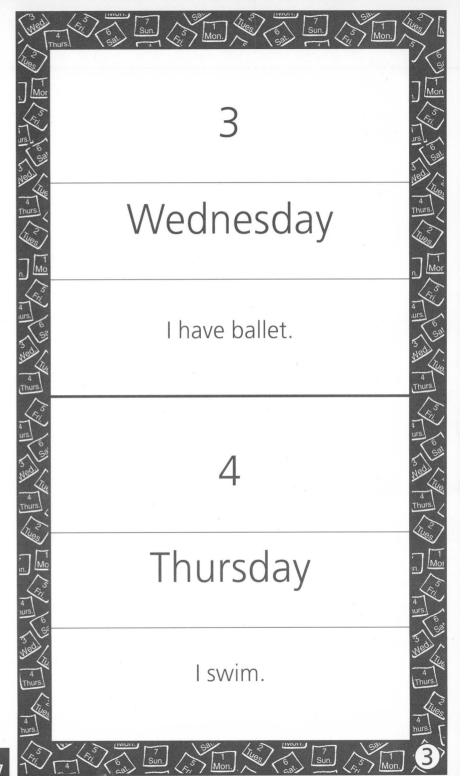

3

Wednesday

I have ballet.

4

Thursday

I swim.

5

Friday

I have gym again.

6

Saturday

I sleep late.

7

Sunday

I'm busy.

_____

(name)

has read the

Snap

story summary to me.

_____

(signed)

Snap

story summary

Snap was a little crocodile.

She liked lots of things.

She liked to eat gingersnaps,

②

snap dancing!

take snapshots,

snap her fingers,

smell snapdragons,

and look snappy.

But most of all, she loved

_____

(name)

has read the

Where Does Everybody Go?

story summary to me.

_____

(signed)

Where Does Everybody Go?

story summary

Where does everybody go
when rain falls and winds blow?

Where do you go
when rain falls and winds blow?

6

When rain falls and winds blow,
the birds go to their nests,

3

the rabbits go to their burrows,

the spiders go under the leaves,

the squirrels go into the trees,

and the foxes go to their dens.

4

5

_____

(name)

has read the

Making a Birdhouse

story summary to me.

_____

(signed)

Making a Birdhouse

story summary

How to make a birdhouse:

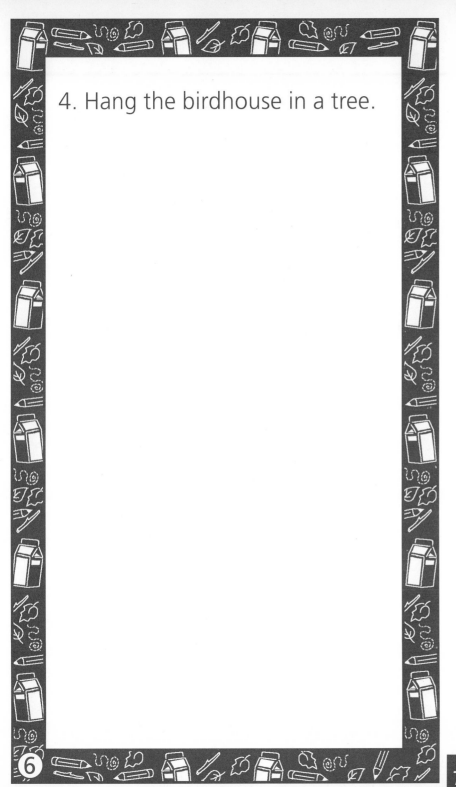

4. Hang the birdhouse in a tree.

6

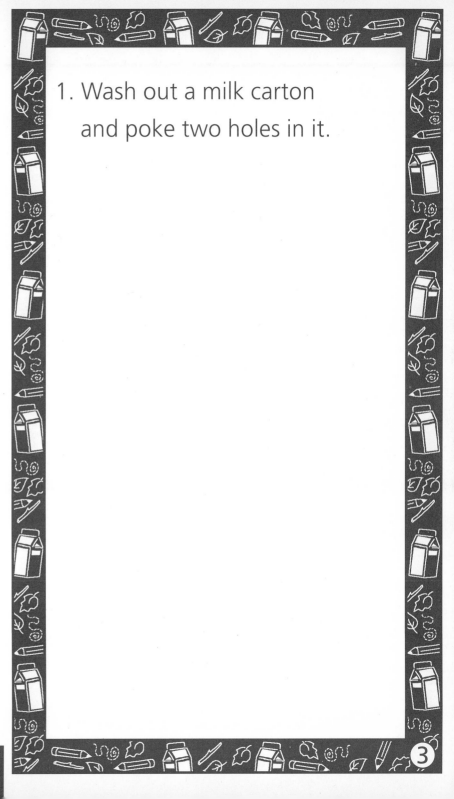

1. Wash out a milk carton and poke two holes in it.

3

2. Put string through the holes and tie the ends together.

3. Glue leaves, grass, or sticks onto the milk carton.

_____

(name)

has read the

Oh, John the Rabbit!

story summary to me.

_____

(signed)

Oh, John the Rabbit!

story summary

I see John the Rabbit . . .

②

grabs all the food in the garden!

6

jumping in the garden,

eating the cabbage,

3

eating the sweet potatoes,
eating the fresh tomatoes.

That John the Rabbit . . .

_____

(name)

has read the

Wheels All Around

story summary to me.

_____

(signed)

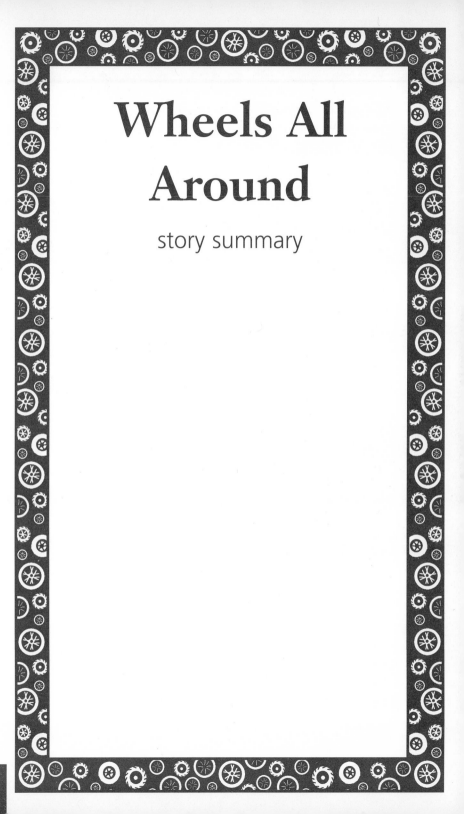

Wheels All Around

story summary

Wheels, wheels,
for work and play.
Little wheels, big wheels
roll all day.

②

Wheels, wheels,
fast and slow,
push and pull,
go, go, go!

6

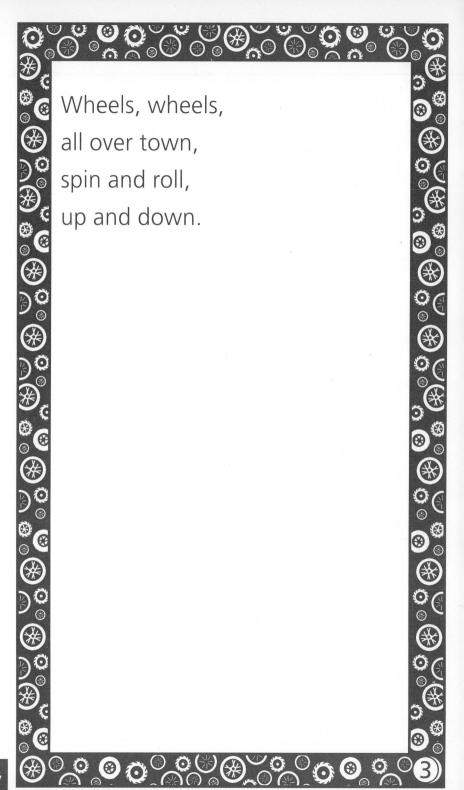

Wheels, wheels,
all over town,
spin and roll,
up and down.

3

Cars and tractors,
trucks and planes,
chairs and bikes,
toys and trains.

Rolling, rolling
here to there,
round and round
everywhere.

_____

(name)

has read the

Brothers

story summary to me.

_____

(signed)

Brothers

story summary

My brother and I have fun together when he comes to visit.

Then the visit is over and
it's time for my brother to go.
The days go by so fast
when my brother visits, but
he always comes back soon.

6

My brother and I
play basketball together
and swim and jump
in the pool.

3

My brother and I
watch movies together
and skate in the park.

④

My brother and I ride
the roller coaster
again and again.

⑤

_____

(name)

has read the

Tiny Bird

story summary to me.

_____

(signed)

Tiny Bird

story summary

The hummingbird is a tiny bird,

for its very tiny babies.

but it drinks from hundreds
of flowers a day
and eats many insects.

The hummingbird is a tiny bird,
but it flies very fast.
Its wings beat very, very fast!

The hummingbird is a tiny bird,
but it builds a strong nest . . .

4

5

_____

(name)

has read the

**Here We Go Round
the Mulberry Bush**

story summary to me.

_____

(signed)

Here We Go Round the Mulberry Bush

story summary

2

Here we go round

    the mulberry bush,

    the mulberry bush,

    the mulberry bush.

Here we go round

    the mulberry bush,

On a cold and frosty morning.

Here we go round

    the mulberry bush,

    the mulberry bush,

    the mulberry bush.

Here we go round

    the mulberry bush,

On a cold and frosty morning.

This is the way we
      wash our hands,
      wash our hands,
      wash our hands.
And this is the way
      we brush our teeth.
And then we wash our faces.

This is the way
      we comb our hair,
      comb our hair,
      comb our hair.
And this is the way
      we wave goodbye.
And then we are on our way
      to school.

4

5

_____

(name)

has read the

Me

story summary to me.

_____

(signed)

Me

story summary

My family says . . .

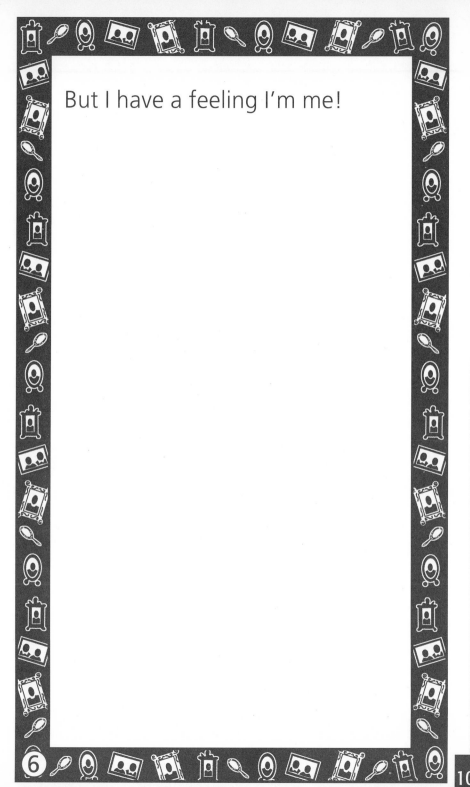

But I have a feeling I'm me!

6

I have my dad's nose
and I have my mom's eyes.

3

They say I have

my sister's hands

and I have my brother's feet.

④

They say I have

my grandpa's legs

and I have my granny's hair.

⑤

_____

(name)

has read the

**There's Nobody
Quite Like Me!**

story summary to me.

_____

(signed)

There's Nobody Quite Like Me!

story summary

There's nobody quite like me!

But there's nobody quite like me!

6

My friend can be exactly
the same height
or have the same sort of hair.

3

My friend can have
the same color eyes
or read exactly the same books.

My friend can like
the same kind of music.
And my twin can even look
exactly like me.

④

⑤

_____

(name)

has read the

I'm the Captain

story summary to me.

_____

(signed)

I'm the Captain

story summary

When a girl pretends she's captain of a ship . . .

She does what she likes best . . .
until it's time to go ashore.

6

She sails upon the sea.

3

She and the crew battle
stormy waves,
and they sail in creepy caves.

They find a treasure chest!

_____

(name)

has read the

One Peaceful Pond

story summary to me.

_____

(signed)

One Peaceful Pond

story summary

Ten tadpoles,
Nine ducks,

Two kingfishers,
One pond!

⑥

Eight reeds,
Seven dragonflies,

③

Six lilies,
Five frogs,

Four fish,
Three water beetles,

_____

(name)

has read

The First Day of School

story summary to me.

_____

(signed)

The First Day of School

story summary

On her first day of school,
a girl made a painting of a tiger
in a tree.

But she really had fun!

She read a big story book.

6

3

Three girls asked to be
her best friend,
and she got an elephant stamp
and a gold star.

At lunch, her sandwiches
were soggy because
the juice leaked.
And she hurt her knees.

④

⑤